A to XP
The Agile ABC Book

written by Karen Favazza Spencer

illustrated by Mary Lou Nye

Agile
Kindergarten

First Edition, 2012
Published by Agile Kindergarten, 67 Langsford Street, Gloucester, MA 01930
Design and layout by MLN Design
Printed in the USA

Spencer, Karen Favazza
Summary: Job aid for Agile transformation and project management in business and software development, including Lean, Scrum and eXtreme Programming practices.

Library of Congress Control Number: 2012918794
ISBN 978-0-9883358-0-6

For more information contact Agile Kindergarten at www.agilekindergarten.com

Table of Contents

Introduction

When you change the way you look at things,
the things you look at change.

~ Max Planck

Intended as a conversation starter for teams
transitioning to Agile, I hope my little book brings a
little clarity to the minds of Agile novices and a little
smile to the lips of Agile old hands.

A is for Agile

Agile is an open and humble mindset.

Agile is an umbrella term that describes a philosophical approach to business development. The goal of Agility is for teams to work collaboratively to eliminate wasted effort and to maximize value to the customer. Agile implementations emphasize continuous improvement, transparent processes and shared responsibility. Increased through-put and quality are the output of all disciplines in the Agile toolbox. A few of the more popular Agile frameworks include:

- Lean — Popular in manufacturing and with business product development

- Scrum — An iterative and incremental approach to software project management

- eXtreme Programing (XP) — A set of collaborative software engineering practices.

agilekindergarten.com

B is for Business Value

A to XP: The Agile ABC Book

MoSCoW:
Must have. Should have.
Could have. Won't have.

Business Value is used in Agile to prioritize work items consistent with the enterprise strategy. Business Value is determined by weighting the importance, urgency and cost of every piece of functionality, and by considering the penalty of inaction.

Although there are helpful formulas that compare the worth of dissimilar work items, understanding how each decision aligns with stakeholder and business goals is central to determining the scope of what must be done to succeed.

agilekindergarten.com

C is for Consensus

Consensus is about resolving conflict collaboratively and respectfully.

Speaking openly is as important as listening with an open mind. Agile methods engage the entire Team in conversation by using clearly defined ceremonies to work through the inevitable conflicts. This dynamic consent process is about living in the present moment with a mindset that steers towards a future goal.

The resolution of every important conflict is a consent decision, meaning all members freely agree to support that decision even if they individually feel another decision is better. The ensuing consensus aligns operations and vision.

agilekindergarten.com

D is for Decision Making

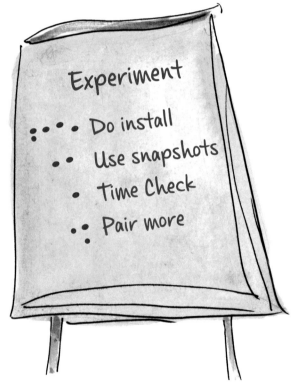

The most important decisions are how to decide and who should decide.

Boundaries around role and responsibility establish the Agile playing field. The rules of the collaborative game played on that field involve two basic decision making processes, maximizing and satisficing. Each has its place in Agile.

1. Maximizing identifies all options and their associated risks. Stakeholders weigh all factors to identify the optimal solution.

2. Satisficing implements the first option that promises to get the job done without concern that there may be better options. Satisficing is an experiential "try it and see" method

E is for Estimating

Estimation reveals details and facilitates planning.

Story Points are a sizing device Agile Teams sometimes use in estimation to engage product management, customers and technical development in requirement conversation. Story Points assign a numerical value to the effort of a piece of work relative to other work in the Product Backlog.

Although arbitrary and variable, Story Points and other sizing devices allow the technical Team to forecast a completion date with approximate certainty. Sizing values provide project predictability. However, Estimation is not a binding contract. Neither are Story Points a measure of performance.

agilekindergarten.com

F is for Feedback Loops

Inspect and Adapt!

By organizing work into short time periods, teams establish a cadence that reflects an iterative and empirical mindset. The time periods are called Sprints in the Scrum framework and last between one and four weeks. At the Sprint boundaries, Scrum teams inspect their product with their stakeholders in a Customer Review and their work processes in a Team Retrospective.

Lean incorporates a Total Quality Management inspection process called Kaizen into the daily manufacturing cycle. This empirical cycle creates a recurring feedback loop that validates or corrects product and process in a natural rhythm consistent with constructivist learning theory.

G is for Greatness

Greatness is never singular.

The inclusive nature of Agile methods encourages the Team to become greater than the sum of its individuals. Cross functional teams with diverse skill sets exhibit more creative problem solving when working in a collaborative environment. Agile businesses honor the powerful synergy that develops on highly productive teams by keeping them intact for long periods of time.

H is for Habituation

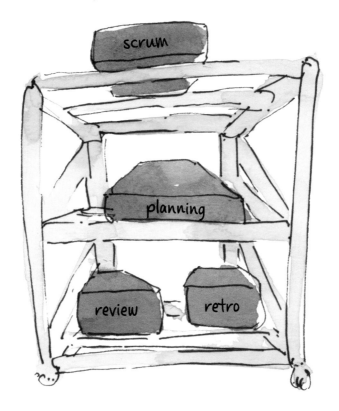

Procedural scaffolding lets us focus on the content.

When a team follows the foundational rules of an Agile framework such as Scrum or XP, they establish solid problem solving habits. These team habits help focus energy on the novel content of the problem, rather than the logistics of dealing with the problem.

Perhaps the best thing about habituation in Agile shops is that Agile is sensitive to both content and context. It encourages creating and discarding habits to maximize effectiveness in service of the people, process and product.

I is for
Information Radiators

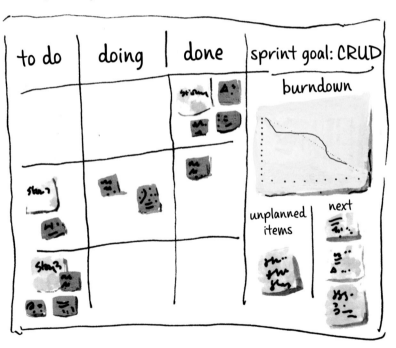

I see and I remember.
I do and I understand
~Proverb

Graphical and interactive, Information Radiators are highly visible charts that broadcast process, progress and priorities at a glance. A form of Visual Management, Information Radiators increase awareness and focus which in turn improve productivity and quality. They have the added benefit of creating a shared space for the team, which synchronizes the team's attitudes as well as behaviors, literally and effortlessly keeping them on the same page.

J is for Just Do It!

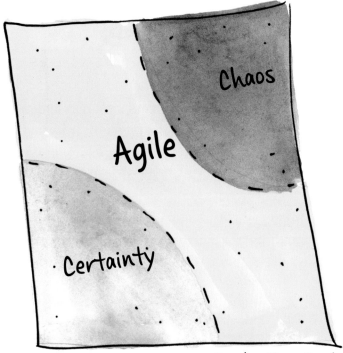

Based on Stacey Graph

It sometimes takes many small failures to achieve a great success.

When the work in Agile environments is sized in small increments that can be completed in short time periods, the cost of failure is also small. Consequently, the teams are able to experiment more, failing fast and often. Trying new things, accepting failure as an opportunity to learn and synthesizing the learning into future endeavors builds stronger products, individuals and teams.

agilekindergarten.com

K is for KISS

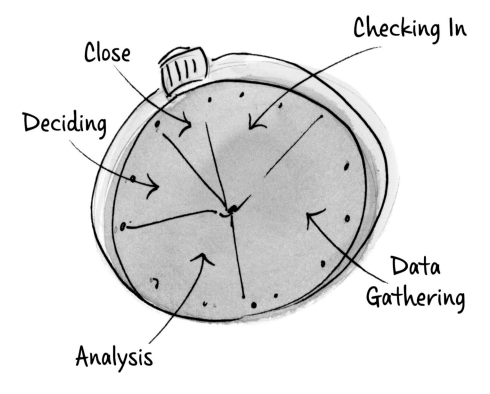

Close

Checking In

Deciding

Data Gathering

Analysis

Keep it short and simple.

Time-boxing, a common practice in Agile, refers to limiting the time spent on a specific activity. Teams decompose features into small and understandable work items that can be completed in one to three days, and work items into tasks that can be completed in hours.

Agile meeting agendas are also time-boxed to logically lead the participants through just enough data gathering and analysis to achieve the meeting goal. By working in these short time frames, work has a higher likelihood of being successfully completed on time.

L is for Lean

> A bad system will beat a
> good person every time.
> ~ W. Edwards Deming

Lean is an approach to work that originated in manufacturing. Lean assumes that every worker contributes as best they can given the constraints of the system in which they operate. Lean engages the entire staff through a variety of highly graphical tools and collaborative team work that emphasizes quality. The worker has input into the modification of the system so as to optimize workflow.

Lean thinking has been widely adopted by business, particularly in the area of Product Management. Continuous Improvement, Kanban, Value Stream Mapping and Pull Processing are Lean concepts.

M is for Measurement

Measure the wrong thing and you get the wrong behaviors.
~ John H. Lingle

Agile emphasizes measuring leading indicators rather than lagging indicators so that actions can be taken to correct course, quickly. For example:

A. Instead of aligning milestones and dates on a Gant chart, Agile predicts project completion based on velocity to adjust scope.

B. Instead of measuring defects from last quarter, Agile tracks the pass rate of tested features to address technical debt.

C. Instead of tracking delivery dates, Agile analyzes the discrepancy between committed and actual dates to remove impediments.

N is for Narrative

TITLE
_____

As a ⟨user⟩

I want ⟨action⟩

so that ⟨business value⟩.

Stories are the operating systems of our minds.

Human beings have told stories to each other since prehistoric times. Stories cement tribes together with a common history and common imagery. Agile uses a narrative device called a "user story" to actively engage the worker in the meaning of each increment of work. The story approach creates a better cognitive understanding of the work and a more satisfying emotional experience.

O is for Ownership

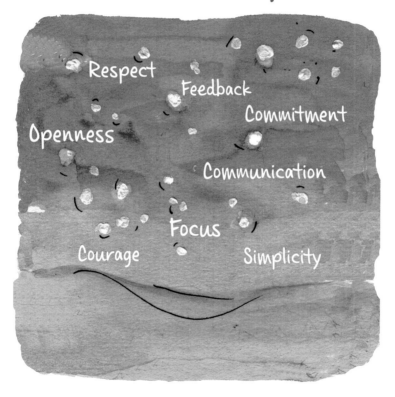

A to XP: The Agile ABC Book

When agreement is necessary to move forward, then participants engage.

Accountability may be one of the biggest differences in an Agile approach to work. Since the Team, rather than the individual, is held accountable for the work product and the Team is expected to make decisions on how they meet their commitments, the Team jointly owns whatever challenges they face. It can be uncomfortable at times, especially in a collaborative and co-located environment. Consequently, Agile puts great emphasis on behaving in a manner consistent with the constellation of team values.

agilekindergarten.com

P is for Planning

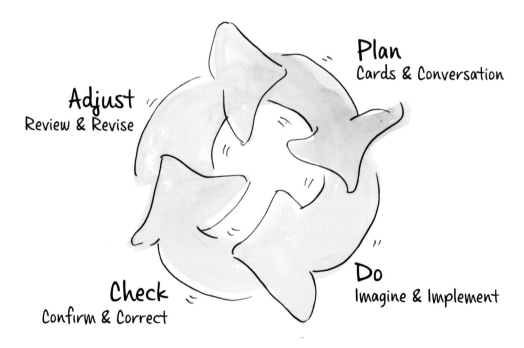

Plan
Cards & Conversation

Adjust
Review & Revise

Do
Imagine & Implement

Check
Confirm & Correct

A to XP: The Agile ABC Book

Continuous Improvement broadens our view and sharpens our focus.

Agile teams plan continuously. In Scrum, every iteration begins with a two part planning session where the Team begins designing functionality and identifying tasks. During the iteration, the Team pairs and swarms to work out the analysis, coding and testing challenges of their work commitment. They also devote 10% of their time to working with the business to understand the work anticipated in the next iteration or two. As a consequence, architectural design emerges in an evolutionary manner as the Team works its way through the iterative cycle.

agilekindergarten.com

Q is for Quality

Acme Chocolates

Input + Process = Output

Agile has its roots in the many quality initiatives of the Industrial Age. From the machinery of Eli Whitney and Henry Ford to the workflows of W. Edwards Deming and Genichi Taguchi, creating quality by developing repeatable processes has powered all Agile frameworks. However, the structures of the past that assumed output was a known quantity do not work in this 21st century Age of Complexity.

Today's context sensitive Agile frameworks replace prescriptive process and management hierarchies with responsive practices and self-management.

R is for Roles

The roles we assume provide us with a compass and baggage.

Our roles dictate our responsibilities and influence our behavior. Scrum teams emphasize power sharing among three roles, each with specific authority and defined boundaries.

A. Product Owner: Prioritizes the work. Owns the Product Backlog. Accepts or rejects the increments built by the team. The voice of the customer.

B. Team: Determines how to solve the business problems. Commits to best engineering and testing practices. Technologists.

C. Scrum Master: Ensures the Agile procedures and philosophy are followed. Removes obstacles that hinder the team. A servant leader.

agilekindergarten.com

S is for Scrum

A to XP: The Agile ABC Book

A Scrum is a daily sharing of what is mutually meaningful.

Scrum is an Agile software development framework. Scrum emphasizes the importance of simple rules for dealing with the recurring elements of any complex project.

The small technical Team holds a daily 15 minute team meeting, called either a Scrum or Stand-Up, to share relevant information. In round robin style, the Team answers three questions concerning what each did since they last met, what each plans on doing before they next meet and identifies any impediments to their progress. Also during the Scrum, the Team updates the task board and burn-down chart to visually broadcast their progress.

agilekindergarten.com

T is for Team

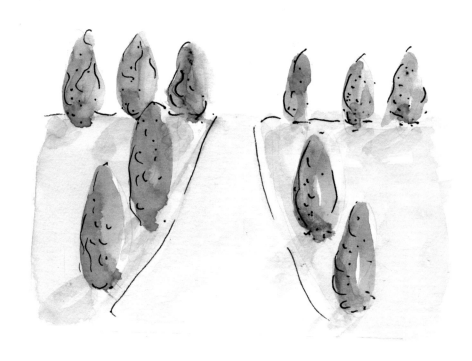

Communication Path = $n(n-1)/2$

Keeping the team roster in the single digits improves communication by limiting the number of communication paths. It's really very simple. When there are five people involved, there are ten communication paths. With ten people involved, there are 45 communication paths.

One of the truisms of systems is Conway's law, which states that technical systems reflect the communication structures of the organizations that build them. Complex organizations tend to create complex and hard-to-maintain technology. Small cross-functional Agile teams with their consensus mentality, frequent meetings and limited roles reduce the multiple communication interfaces that are common in traditional approaches.

agilekindergarten.com

U is for Users

There are no solutions, just stories.
~ Garrison Keillor

Above all else, Agile is a common sense approach to work that emphasizes the user perspective and the user benefit. At the beginning of each project, Agile teams develop Personas to represent their users. Teams detail persona demographics, specific needs and underlying goals. Teams further humanize their Personas with names and photos or drawings.

Functional business tests are based on the Acceptance Criteria from each User Story written as a Persona request. By keeping the user topmost in their minds, the Team is better equipped to assist the business in delivering the best possible product.

V is for Velocity

performance

time

Velocity varies, but productivity trends upwards in Agile projects.

Velocity refers to the work a team typically is expected to complete in an iteration. Velocity is sometimes expressed as a range of Story Points based on the team average for the project, such as an average Velocity of 34, with an expected range of 29 to 46.

Velocity is about probability, not promises. Velocity trends provide a window into the health of Agile Teams. When a team is supported by an Agile Coach in an Agile environment, velocity variation exhibits a J-Curve pattern. The short periodic plateaus, steep upticks and an overall upward trend of the J-Curve indicates a sustainable and learning culture.

agilekindergarten.com

W is for White Boards

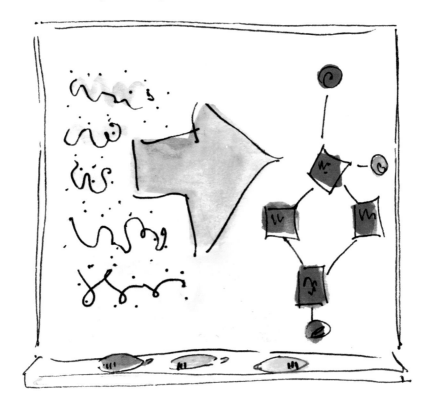

One picture is worth a hundred page specification document.

Whiteboard discussions allow teams to collaborate while being literally on the same page. Using a shared space increases both individual and collaborative brain power. Moreover, thinking aloud on a whiteboard engages the sensory as well as the reasoning portions of our brains. Externalizing the content this way allows us to focus our mental energies on specific points in a complicated process, without simultaneously having to remember all the detail.

XP is for
eXtreme Programming

Disciplined engineering practices provide the foundations of success.

eXtreme Programming (XP) stitches together technical aspects of software development and group dynamics to create an organizational culture. XP emphasizes best practices, such as pair programming, unit testing, test driven design, acceptance test driven development, test automation, refactoring and self-organizing teams. All Agile frameworks recognize the disciplined, yet agile, XP engineering approaches as integral to successful software development.

Y is for Why?

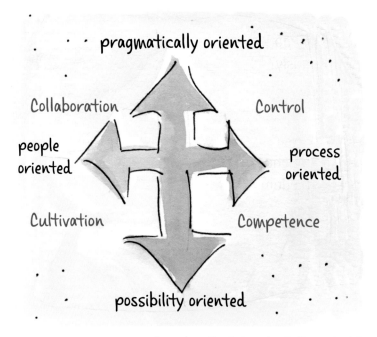

pragmatically oriented

Collaboration

Control

people
oriented

process
oriented

Cultivation

Competence

possibility oriented

Based on the Schneider Culture Model

A to XP: The Agile ABC Book

Agile teams are incubators for leaders.

At every level, Agile asks why. Why is the story important to the user? Why do we refactor a piece of code? Why do we test continuously? Why do we chose to work in this messy and challenging manner?

We chose Agile because Agile frameworks create a humanistic work culture in a sustainable and evolving enterprise ecosystem. We chose Scrum, Lean and XP because they encourage freedom of thought and action. Agile cultivates professionalism and growth. Agile is a transformative experience on a personal, team and enterprise level.

Z is for Zero Defects

It is not done until it is defect free.

Defects are expected, but the pragmatic Agile processes and experiential mindset have a profound effect on defect handling. It begins with the team Definition of Done (DoD). Definition of Done applies to work at the story level, sprint level and release level. One of the criteria for DoD at any level is "defect free." Consequently, the team determines how to dispatch defects as rapidly and as pragmatically as possible.

How to Use this Book

Think of A to XP as a Sudoku puzzle. Some of the answers are provided, but you need to figure out the missing pieces. And you need to do it with your team.

Step 1

    A. Choose a concept that is challenging your team.

    B. Find the appropriate letter.

    C. Break your team into pairs or groups of three to discuss one or two of the four components of that letter:

- the image title
- the image
- the quote
- the text.

agilekindergarten.com

Step 2

Ask and answer a few Powerful Questions:

      A. What would make our practice better?
      B. What other angles can we think of?
      C. How do we want it to be?
      D. If we had it, what would we have?
      E. What do we feel most about this?
      F. What resonates?
      G. What is most interesting?
      H. How might this play out in our environment?
      I. Whose problem is this?
      J. What would this look like on an Agile team?
      K. What does this look like on our team?
      L. What have we not tried doing, yet?

Record your answers and insights on flip chart paper.

A to XP: The Agile ABC Book

Step 3

Come back together as a team. Tour each of the flip chart lists. Each member identifies his top three ideas from all of the charts.

A. Create a new flip chart list of the top ideas chosen by the team.

B. Then, as a team, ask the hard question:

   ■ What steps can we take to get from where we are to where we want to be?

C. Create Action Items that can be implemented by the team.

Index

About the Author

Karen Favazza Spencer is an Agile Coach living in Gloucester, Massachusetts and serving clients nationally. A former kindergarten teacher, Karen claims she learned most of what she needed to know about project management and teamwork in kindergarten. For more about Karen or to order more copies of **A to XP: The Agile ABC Book**, visit www.AgileKindergarten.com.

About the Illustrator

Mary Lou Nye designed and illustrated **A to XP**. When not doing graphics, she designs gardens. Mary Lou and her dog Molly live on Cape Ann, a place of great inspiration to both. You can see more of her work at www.marylounye.net.